dream

dictionary

WHAT YOUR DREAMS MEAN

BY SUSAN MAGEE

Lawrence Teacher Books
Philadelphia

Mechanicals produced by book soup publishing, inc.

Interior design by Maria Taffera Lewis
@ Blue Studio Design

All photography © 2001 by Photonica

Edited by Erin Slonaker

ISBN 1-930408-20-X
10 9 8 7 6 5 4 3 2 1

Please support your local book or gift store.
However, if you cannot find this book there,
you may order it directly from the publisher.
Please add $1.50 for postage and handling.
Send check or money order to the address below.

Lawrence Teacher Books
1 Pearl Buck Court
Bristol, PA 19007

INTRODUCTION

If you're baffled by your dreams, you're
not alone. Humans have been trying to
figure out what dreams mean for as long
as we've been dreaming.

Dreams, even the most confusing,
ridiculous, and illogical ones, do offer
us clues as to what they are saying.
The meaning of dreams has always been
thought to reside within the symbols
they conjure.

For centuries, dream interpretation

looked at these symbols through a superstitious eye. In the twentieth century, thanks largely to the work of psychiatrists Sigmund Freud and Carl Jung, people began to look at dreams and dream symbols as a potential window to one's unconscious mind.

This little book can be a starting place for your journey into your dream world—think of it as a guide, a starting point, a place to gain inspiration. Keep in mind that while the symbols gathered here are the most common dream symbols, no one person or dictionary can tell you for certain what a dream symbol means—you have to figure that out yourself.

So read on, and discover the secrets within your mind. May all your dreams be sweet—but if perchance they are not, may you at least learn to unravel their mysteries. . . .

A

ACCIDENT

Can indicate a fear of failure, anxiousness about change, or recklessness. May be a warning to be more careful.

AIRPLANE

If you are afraid of flying, you may be apprehensive about the future. If you are the pilot, it may indicate a desire or an opportunity for self-expression.

ALIEN

May represent an ignored or unknown aspect of your personality that you need to become more familiar with. You may secretly want to explore new ideas.

A

ANGELS

You may be on the brink of profound change: whether it's good or bad depends upon the feeling the dream gives you. Angels may come to us in dreams to deliver important messages.

ANGER

If you're the angry person in the dream,
you may, in fact, be angry in your
waking life and not realize it. Dream
anger can also mean that you are
frustrated or disappointed about
something. If someone is angry with
you, you may be feeling guilty.

ANIMALS

An instinct, a personality trait, or an
unmet physical need may be bubbling

A

to the surface when you dream of animals. Consider the specific qualities that make each animal unique, or certain behavior that is characteristic for the animal: you may desire these qualities yourself.

A

APPLE

May have less to do with food and more to do with knowledge—general or self. You may need to be wiser or to seek out new information or ideas.

ATTACK

If you're the attacker, you may be
expressing frustration with a situation or
problem you're facing in your waking
life. If you're attacking a person, you
may have uncomfortable feelings about a
real person in your life. If you're
attacking an object, it may represent a
situation or place where the problem lies.

AUTOMOBILE

May mean it's time to pursue your goals

A

and ambitions. Being alone in an
automobile may signify that you have
self-confidence and independence,
unless you feel lost or afraid. If someone
else is driving, you may be realizing
that someone has too much influence
over you, making you unhappy. On the
other hand, if you are happy to be
driven by this person, you welcome a
relationship or partnership.

A

B

BABY

May symbolize a new beginning. Can also indicate that some aspect of your personality is underdeveloped. Can represent feelings of vulnerability. It could also be more literal—a desire to start a family.

BAKING

If you are baking, you may be feeling creative or the need to be more creative.

BABY

If there is a baker in your dream, he or
she may represent how you see your
creative self.

B

BARBER OR BEAUTICIAN

You may desire a change in your
physical appearance or your situation.

BATH

May indicate a desire to come clean
about a secret or something unpleasant.
Could also mean that old feelings are

now washed away and that you've had a change of heart.

BEACH

Because the sea is thought to represent the unconscious mind, the beach can be the symbolic place where the conscious and the unconscious meet. Dreaming of a beach could mean you stand on the threshold of profound change or transformation or you simply need a vacation.

B

BEES

Ancient cultures believed this was favorable, predicting peace and wealth. The saying, "As busy as a bee" offers another interpretation—your mind is busy and productive or needs to be.

B

BIRDS

You may discover how you feel about a relationship in your life through birds in your dream. Consider what the particular bird is known for. An owl

may suggest that you need more
knowledge about the person or the
relationship. Birds in flight may
represent a higher intelligence.

BLOOD

B

Blood in dreams often holds positive
meaning—it's your life force. Bleeding
can be a desire to release passions or
indicate that a person or situation is
draining you. To drink or exchange
blood can mean a desire for union.

BOOKS

You may be seeking knowledge or the
answer to a problem if you see or read a
book, or visit a library.

B

BRIDGE

A powerful dream symbol that is best
understood by the feeling you have
when looking at or crossing the bridge.
If you are fearful, it can signal danger—
the possibility of falling into an abyss. If
you feel safe and self-confident, it can

signal transformation—the crossing of a
threshold, a boundary, or reaching a
new level of consciousness.

BULL

May represent your sexual instincts
and/or your creative energies.

BUTTERFLY

Generally thought to be a positive
symbol of the self, indicating that you
are fully evolved and released. Can also

B

represent a desire for independence. You may not be ready to "settle down."

BUTTONS

B

To dream about wearing clothing with many buttons may mean that you feel overwhelmed or restrained by societal values or expectations. To lose a button can mean that you have violated a moral code. To unbutton buttons may signify that you want to more fully express yourself.

C

CAGE

You may have some inhibitions that are
holding you back. If the cage seems
more like a fence, or you feel good, it
can be a positive symbol, meaning that
you feel protected and safe.

CASTLE

A castle is thought to represent your
sense of security. If too well-protected,

your defense mechanisms could keep others away. If it's crumbling or under siege, you may be too vulnerable. If the castle is a positive place, some sense of security—positive self-protection—may have been reached.

CAT

On the one hand, the cat can be a symbol of cunning or deceit. On the other hand, it can be a strong feminine symbol of independence, wisdom, and imagination. For a man, it might mean that he needs to be more in touch with his feminine side.

CHAIN

Something may be holding you back, most likely some kind of dependency.

CHASE

If you are being chased, you may be trying to escape responsibility, or you have strong emotions you do not want to

face. Some dream analysts believe that if
you turn toward your pursuer, your fear
may go away. If you're the chaser, you
may be frustrated or feeling thwarted in
pursuing your dreams.

CHOKING

You may be experiencing generalized
anxiety in your waking life that spills
over to your dream state. You may feel
choked, cut off, unable to breathe freely
because of a condition in your life.

CLIMBING

On a practical level, it can indicate success or the desire for success. For Freud, climbing symbolized sexual desires. Jung believed it was a desire to reach one's higher or spiritual self.

CLOTHES

Your feelings about your persona are often expressed in dreams through clothing. If you're inappropriately dressed or underdressed, you may be

worried that you are not capable of
performing a task. Being over-dressed
may mean that your public face is too
disconnected from your private one.
Clothes that are too tight may mean that
your public role is too inhibiting. Being
caught in your undergarments is often
an expression of shame.

COFFIN

Though associated with funerals, coffins
are often positive dream symbols. Some

bad, old, or unnecessary part of our lives or selves has been killed off and will now be buried. It could indicate a new beginning.

COLORS

Color can hold significance, especially if it is notable in some way. Red can express passion, anger, or sexual arousal. Orange can signify hope, new beginnings, or the dawning of spiritual understanding. Yellow can mean authority and power.

CUP

Green, the color of nature, may indicate rebirth. Blue is a highly spiritual dream color, though it could indicate depression, as in "the blues." Gold is the color of the sun and can signify consciousness. Brown may express feelings about nature and physical reality.

C

CUP

Stands for love and truth. If the cup holds wine, it may reveal your attitude about religion or spirituality.

D

DANCING

Dancing can express desire for creative freedom or sexual fulfillment.

DEATH

In early dream interpretation, death meant bad news, illness, or great disappointment was on the horizon. The modern view of death says that the old is dying off, making way for the new.

DECEASED LOVED ONE

You may simply miss the person. Or,
you may have unresolved feelings about
the person that you are attempting to
work out in your dreams.

D

DESERT

You may be lonely or isolated.

DEVIL

If you dream about devils, demons,
witches, or monsters you may be

dreaming about unpleasant aspects of
your own personality. Jung felt the
dreamer should consciously acknowledge the uncomfortable feelings.

D

DIVING

You may want to literally "get to the
bottom" of a current situation or
emotion.

DOCTOR

You may need physical or emotional

healing. Because doctors are seen as knowledgeable people who give us guidance and advice, they may represent your own source of inner wisdom.

DOG

D

Often, how you feel about friendships is revealed by dogs. If the dog is friendly, it can represent devotion. If the dog is unfriendly or dangerous, it could mean that a person in your life has those qualities. Dogs can also mean you are

under the influence of misused or
neglected instincts.

DOOR

D

In early dream interpretation, going
through a door, unless it belonged to
one's childhood home, was a portent for
bad news. Today, it is viewed as a more
positive symbol—something new is on
your horizon. But if you cannot open the
door, you may be feeling repressed or
fearful of the unknown.

DROWNING

Can mean that you are overwhelmed by something in your unconscious mind or that you feel threatened by events or situations in your life.

DWARF OR ELF

A dwarf, elf, or midget could be a magical messenger from your unconscious mind. He or she can appear in dreams to remind us of our own unexplored creative powers and resources.

D

E

EAR/EARRING

May represent how well you listen. You may need to pay greater attention.

EARTHQUAKE

May mean that you're angry, have self-destructive feelings, or are experiencing emotional upheaval. Or it could signify a desire to shake things up, to find a new way of doing something.

EATING

Often represents a need for physical or emotional nourishment.

EGG

Freud believed an egg symbolized female fertility, motherhood, and sexuality. Jung believed that dream eggs held our captive souls. Eggs can also be symbolic of a new beginning or rebirth. Because eggshells are so fragile, they could mean that you have a delicate

E

situation that needs careful handling.

EIGHT

Commonly associated with the Buddha, this number can be a symbol of spirituality, the divine, or new beginnings.

ELEPHANT

In Hindu-Buddhist mythology, the elephant is a sacred symbol of self-knowledge and wisdom, and it may have the same meaning in your dream.

E

ELEVATORS

If trapped in one, this may indicate an
inferiority complex. If the elevator is
moving up, it could signify advancement
and realization of your goals. If the
elevator is moving down, this may
indicate a fear of letting go.

EX-BOYFRIENDS/GIRLFRIENDS/
LOVERS/SPOUSES

You may miss the person. You may not
have emotionally let go of the

relationship. You may be dreaming about aspects of yourself that you're projecting onto the person.

E

EYES

Bright, large eyes suggest a healthy spiritual life. Closed, tearful, or red eyes may indicate a sad or needy spiritual state. Eyeglasses may signify a need to see a situation or person more clearly.

F

FALLING

It's a very common expression of anxiety to fall in one's dreams. You may be feeling insecure, threatened, or afraid to let something go.

FAMOUS PEOPLE

Why is the person famous? You may want to have the same quality. You may also discover an aspect of your own

F

personality that you don't like or are
unfamiliar with.

FATHER

May simply be your father. Or he may
symbolize a need for wisdom or
maturity. If a woman dreams about her
father she may be exploring her
masculine qualities. (See MAN.)

FIRE

May represent passionate or consuming

FIRE

emotions. Could be a warning to stop
engaging in negative or destructive
behavior. Fire also cleanses and purifies,
so it may indicate a desire to start fresh.

F

FISH

In Christianity, fish symbolize the divine.
They may represent your spiritual state,
personal growth, or insights into your
unconscious mind. Fish caught in a net
and brought to the surface may be
unconscious thoughts coming to light.

FLIES

A swarm of flies may represent a frustrating or annoying person or situation in your life that you need to escape.

FLOATING

F

If you are peacefully drifting in the air or on water, this means you feel peaceful. If you are unhappy to be floating, you may feel unresolved or not grounded about something in your waking life.

FLOWER

A symbol of the self. If the flower is in
bloom, so is your true nature. If the
flower is withered or closed, you may be
feeling repressed or unhappy.

F

FLYING

If you're happy and confident in flight,
you may feel free, released, transformed.
You may have reached a new level of
conscious awareness. If you feel afraid or
unsure of yourself, it could symbolize

that you're trying to escape from
problems in your life.

FOG

Fog or smoke may signify confusion.
You are not seeing a situation clearly.

F

FOREST/JUNGLE

Represents unknown aspects of the
unconscious. If you feel lost or afraid in
the woods, you may be afraid of your
thoughts. If you are happy, you are

receptive to your unconscious thoughts.
Can indicate a willingness to explore the
unknown and to take new risks.

FOX

F

Known for cunning and intelligence, a
fox may be telling you to draw on your
analytical qualities rather than emotions
to deal with a situation in your own life.

G

GARBAGE

May represent aspects of your life or your personality that you want to discard. If it is in a bag or a can, you may have already taken steps toward a new beginning.

GARDEN

In folklore, to dream of a garden is good luck. Can represent a loss of innocence,

51

as happened to Adam and Eve. If the garden needs care and nurturing, you may be needy as well.

GIANT

May indicate an inferiority complex or self-doubt. Could also be telling you that someone in your life is trying to dominate you.

GLASS

Often reflects your attitudes about yourself and your sense of wholeness. If it is whole or clear, so is your sense of self. If it is shattered or clouded, you may need emotional or physical attention.

G

GLOVE

You may be seeking protection or covering up your true feelings.

GRANDFATHER/GRANDMOTHER

You may be dreaming of the actual family member. On the other hand, any

elderly man or woman may mean that
you are connecting with a symbolic Wise
Old Man or Woman—your own inner
wisdom, inner healer.

G GUN

Could indicate aggressive feelings—you
may want to take something by force.
Depending on the nature of the dream,
it could be a warning to protect yourself
from a person or situation.

H

HAIR

A symbol of power. Folklorists believed that baldness was a warning about bad health or bad luck. The meaning, however, may be more practical, indicating a lack of something or anxiety, especially if the dream is about losing hair. A full head of hair, long locks, or a beard can all be symbols of vitality.

HANDS

If you're washing your hands, you may feel guilty about something. If you're working with your hands, you may be trying to solve a problem or use skills you don't know you have. To have one's hands tied or bound is a negative symbol that something has you symbolically feeling restricted.

HAT

Suggests you may be playing a role or

H

changing one. If the hat doesn't fit or it
blows off, you may be uncomfortable
with a role you're playing.

HORSE

In Celtic mythology, the horse
symbolizes fertility. A horse in your
dream is considered a sexual symbol or
an indication that you're emotionally
strong. You may be discovering your
own powers or congratulating yourself
for coping well during a difficult time.

HOTEL

A temporary dwelling that may suggest a temporary, or transitional, period.

HOUSE

The various rooms of a house represent the various levels of your psychological and emotional state. Your spiritual development and progress is represented in the highest room—the attic. If the attic is comfortable, you may have reached a new level of spiritual awareness. If the attic is unfinished or in need of repair, your spiritual state may require some attention. Your unconscious mind is represented by the lowest room in a house. It may mean that something you're repressing or ignoring is trying to come into your consciousness. Can also signify that you should follow your instincts. The living room and bedrooms often represent your conscious life and attitudes.

H

ICE

I

ICE

You may have some emotional issues that are frozen within you—you don't want to deal with them. Skating on ice—without falling—can signify that you are dealing with difficult emotional issues well.

ILLNESS

The unconscious mind may give clues to

physical ills even before symptoms are present. Consider how you feel physically and emotionally. Dream illness can also symbolize a wish to be cared for and nurtured.

I

INSECT
Something may literally be bugging or irritating you.

INTRUDER
Can mean that you feel violated or

trespassed upon by someone you know.
Could also be that some unconscious
desire or repressed feeling is forcing
itself upon your consciousness.

ISLAND (DESERTED)

Can mean you feel isolated and lonely.
On the other hand, if you are content
upon your island, it could mean you
want solitude or rest.

J

JELLYFISH

May be a message to be on your guard.
It could be that a scheme is afoot to
injure or sting you.

JOURNEY

Indicates a change in circumstance. The
details are important: if the voyage is
pleasant, all is OK; if the road is rocky
or weather stormy, take care.

JOY

A sign of good health.

JUDGE

A sign of obstacles. Difficulties ahead
if the judge rules against you. If you
are acquitted, you'll get a big fortune.

JURY

Considered unfortunate, but if you're
merely observing a jury, it's a sign that
you'll overcome obstacles.

J

K

KEY

Could be a message from your unconscious that you are about to solve a problem or that you have the ability to unlock inner wisdom.

KING

A king may represent your father or you may be dreaming about a larger, more symbolic father figure. (See FATHER, MAN.)

KITE

You may have a specific creative goal
that you want to release.

KNIFE

If not used as a weapon, which indicates
aggression or hostility, a knife can
symbolize a division in the dreamer's life
or emotional state. On a positive note, a
knife can represent "truth," as in a
cutting away of something false. Freud
felt it was a sexual symbol.

K

L

LADDER

Tells how you are doing in pursuit of a goal. If you're going up, you may be close to attaining it. If you're going down, you may not be moving ahead. A shaky ladder may indicate that you're afraid to pursue your goals. Missing rungs might say that you are missing something that you need to pursue or fulfill your goals.

LEGS

Symbolize your support system. Can signify feelings of power (strong, shapely) or powerlessness (weak, uneven).

LIGHT

L

Whether it's from the sun, a lamp, or candle, light can mean you have reached a new level of understanding or are close to solving a problem. Jung believed light symbolized the conscious mind and that profound insight was occurring.

LIGHTNING

You may be about to receive a flash of illumination or insight. Remember, when it strikes, lightning can be deadly and destructive, so take warning not to make hasty decisions based on the insight the bolt of lightning brings.

LION

To see a lion in your dream usually indicates that great personal success is coming your way.

L

LIQUOR

You may want to lose your inhibitions.

LOCK

You may feel frustrated in solving a
problem or establishing a relationship.
Can also indicate that your feelings are
locked up—open up and explore them.

LUGGAGE

May refer to the dreamer's emotional
baggage.

L

M

MAN

When a woman dreams about a man, whether she knows him or not, he may represent some masculine qualities she should possess. A man dreaming about a man may be dreaming about aspects of himself. (See FATHER.)

MAP

If you can read or follow the map, it's

likely a positive sign that you're on the right path in life. If the map is confusing and hard to read, you might feel like you need guidance or help.

M

MERMAID

A powerful symbol of the feminine, representing inner wisdom. If a man dreams about a mermaid, he may need to get in touch with his more feminine qualities. Or, he may fear his feminine qualities will drown his masculine side.

If a woman dreams of mermaids, she may be thinking about her feminine powers and wisdom.

MILK

In early dream interpretation, drinking milk was a positive omen of wealth and abundant harvests. Today, milk is commonly seen as a symbol of nurturing and/or nourishment. Milk also has connotations of one's mother—you may need to be mothered.

MERMAID

M

MIRROR

If you look in a mirror and see an unfamiliar face, you may be having an identity crisis or be noticing an unfamiliar quality in yourself.

MONEY

You may be dreaming of power or sex.

MONKEYS

Often your playful, mischievous side is represented by this animal.

MOTHER

Can represent your feelings about your mother, but may also be a more symbolic mother figure or Earth Mother who represents creativity, intuition, and that which is unconscious. (See WOMAN.)

MOUTH

Freud considered a mouth to be a sexual symbol. However, it could simply mean a desire to speak out, to communicate, or that a part of you feels repressed.

M

MURDER

May have less to do with violence and more to do with a desire to see a part of yourself, such as a quality or trait, figuratively killed off.

MUSEUM

You may be dreaming or thinking about your past. You may have some unresolved issues from years ago that you thought were solved.

N

NAIL (THE HARDWARE)

Symbolizes bonding or joining. It could mean that you are holding on or holding things together.

NECK

Since it connects the head with the heart, the neck may symbolize uncertainty about which to use—emotions or logic—to solve a problem.

NIGHT

A dream of night or darkness could indicate that you're confronting delays or obstacles, or you may feel lost.

NINE

The numeric symbol of fertility. It can represent a desire to reproduce or a desire for productivity.

NOOSE

A noose is a negative symbol that can

mean you fear something. It could be a fear of being trapped, self-expression, or advancement.

NOSE

May be a message to follow your nose. But if you have a dream in which your nose has grown, it could mean that you, like Pinocchio, need to be more honest.

NUDITY

If you're naked and not concerned about

it, this may be a positive symbol of self-acceptance. It may also be a message from your unconscious that it's okay to reveal your true self to others. If you are anxious, you may feel anxious in real life. Seeing others naked can mean that you're discovering who others really are.

N

NUN

May, depending upon your individual situation, symbolize repressed desires or a need to be more moral.

O

OCEAN

Jung considered the ocean or the sea to
be a profound symbol of the unconscious. Carefully consider how you
feel in or near the ocean. Do you see a
shark fin approaching? This could mean
you're afraid or wary about unconscious
thoughts surfacing. If you're peacefully
swimming or floating, then you may be
ready to integrate unconscious thoughts

into your waking life. The ocean almost always represents strong emotions or emotional energy.

OCTOPUS

May represent feelings about one's mother. Its meaning can also be more literal—you may feel entangled in a situation or by a person in a negative way. You could also feel that you have many different things going on in your life at once.

OFFICER

Getting arrested may mean that you feel you've violated some moral code of conduct or have gone against traditional societal expectations.

ONE

Symbolic of unity, freedom, and independence.

ORCHESTRA

Depending upon the behavior and

sounds produced by the players, this
may be a symbol of harmony or discord
in your emotional life.

OVEN

A symbol for the womb. May reveal
your thoughts and attitudes about
pregnancy. Can also be a symbol for the
birth of new ideas or attitudes.

OWL

Represents your inner wisdom.

P

PACKAGE

May mean that you're on the verge of
solving a problem. If you're sending
the package, you are giving away a
part of yourself. Receiving means you're
getting in touch with an unfamiliar part
of yourself.

P

PAINTING/PICTURE

If the image is of you or another person,

there may be something you need to see about yourself or them. If you are painting, you may have unexplored creative abilities, the desire to approach a situation from a fresh angle, or insight that others around you do not have.

P

PAJAMAS

Being in public in your PJ's can mean that you feel unprepared, inadequate, or unable to meet traditional societal expectations. It could be a more positive symbol that you are willing to break away from tradition and become more creative.

PARKING LOT/GARAGE

Since driving in automobiles reflects journeys, a parking lot represents a pause on that journey, which could be seen as positive or negative. Are you parked, stuck from moving forward? Or, do you feel like you are taking a break or resting from pursuing a goal?

PATH

PATH

The condition of the path reveals its
meaning. Is it a smooth path with no
obstacles? You're going in the right
direction in life. If there are obstacles,
then it could mean that you need to
rethink the direction in which you're
headed. A path that leads downward is
not necessarily negative; you could be
thinking about something very deeply or
exploring previously unexplored
thoughts, ideas, or creative energies.

P

PEARL

To dream of a pearl is to dream of your true self. It can mean that you've achieved or are about to achieve wisdom, great self-expression, or full self-realization.

P

PIT

You may be afraid of something in your waking life—watch out for pitfalls. Can also be the ego fearing being overtaken by unconscious thoughts.

POCKET

You may want to own or possess
something. Could be a hint that there's
some knowledge, resources, or memory
that can help you solve a problem.

P

PRIEST

Depending upon your personal associa-
tions, a priest may offer spiritual
guidance or remind you of your own
sources of inner wisdom. Or you may
feel guilty about something.

Q

QUEEN

Usually a mother symbol representing feelings about your own mother or a larger, more archetypal mother figure. (See MOTHER, WOMAN.)

QUICKSAND

A sign that you may feel pulled down or threatened by a situation, person, or thoughts in your waking life.

QUILL

You may want to express or say something. If you're writing, it may mean that you are about to gain new understanding or knowledge.

QUILT

You may need to piece things together from different sources to solve a problem. A quilt can also indicate a need for warmth—or a desire to cover something up.

R

RABBIT

A white rabbit may be associated with Easter and rebirth. It can also stand for a physical preoccupation with sex or represent fertility in the sense of personal growth.

RAILROAD STATION

A symbol for a spiritual journey or a desire to travel.

RAIN

Can be a symbol of new growth. An emotional or spiritual cleansing may be occurring. If the rain is destructively heavy or causes flooding, you may have strong, possibly upsetting, emotions you need to deal with.

RAINBOW

Almost always a positive symbol of good luck, prosperity, and redemption.

R

RATS

You may feel overrun by a negative or dangerous situation in your life. If they don't upset you, you may be successfully dealing with negative feelings or a negative situation.

RESCUE

If you are rescued by someone in your dream, you may want to let someone else be in control or take responsibility in your life or relationship.

R

ROCK

Can represent stability or a sense of
security. On the negative side, it may be
an obstacle that needs to be overcome.

ROLLER COASTER

You may feel out of control or feel like
your emotions are going up and down.
Conversely, it could be a nudge for you
to have fun, take risks.

R

S

SCHOOL

A school can represent your feelings about career or public morals. You may have professional or social concerns pressing upon you. It could also mean that you have some learning to do.

SEX

You may be wanting to have sex in your waking life. Or it can represent a desire to release unconscious creative energies.

SHARK

May be a memory or desire that you are
afraid to consciously acknowledge.

SHELL

May be a notice to listen to your own
thoughts.

SMOKE

You are unable to see something clearly.

SNAKE

Because it sheds its skin, a snake is a symbol of rebirth. In many Eastern traditions, the snake symbolizes creative life and sexual energy. Expect a burst of creativity, wisdom, or rebirth to occur in your life.

SNOW

Might be telling you something about your views on purity, depending on the quality of the snow.

SNAKE

SPIDERS

Thought to foretell good luck. Spiders are productive, always weaving webs. Perhaps this is a signal for you to get busy. Spiders are also symbols of creativity. Freud believed that spiders represented your feelings—often negative—about your mother.

STAGE

You may have a desire to reveal yourself or take risks.

S

STICKS

May represent aspects of ourselves that
have splintered off or gotten lost.

SUN

(S)

Symbolizes your conscious mind. Is
the sun rising or setting, blinding you,
or warming you? Think about how it
makes you feel in the dream. (See LIGHT,
LIGHTNING.)

T

TEETH

A common anxiety dream people have is
that their teeth are loose, broken, or
falling out. You may fear that you've lost
control. If you are chewing or having
difficulty chewing, you may be unable to
digest or accept new information.

TEMPLE OR CHURCH

Represents your spiritual center, your

religious values. Consider the condition of the structure: If the temple is in good condition, it may be a symbol that your spiritual life is in order, and you are at ease spiritually.

T

TESTS

Finding that you have to take a test and aren't prepared is a common anxiety dream. Test-taking often relates to how ready you feel to meet professional challenges.

THIRST

May indicate actual thirst—but if, upon waking, you're not thirsty, you may be dissatisfied with some aspect of your life.

T

THREE

The number three can represent a total harmony of self—body, mind, and spirit.

TOILET

You may be expressing feelings of embarrassment or shame. Trying to find

a toilet may mean frustration and the
need to express yourself more fully.

TORNADO

Suggests a whirlwind of emotions on
the part of the dreamer.

TWO

A rich symbol that can mean duality or
indicate that a balance has been
achieved. It can signify the joining of
male and female characteristics.

U

UMBRELLA

You may feel you need protection. You may be trying to shield yourself from emotions, realizations, or difficult truths.

UNDERGROUND

You could be keeping feelings or emotions repressed. You can also be discovering new ideas and creative abilities.

UNDRESSING

Can indicate a willingness to show
others who you really are—or a fear of
the same, depending upon how you feel
in the dream.

U

UNIFORM

May mean you fear a loss of individual-
ity. Could also indicate difficulty dealing
with authority figures.

V

VEIL

May mean that you are you hiding something, or that something you need is being hidden or withheld from you.

VOLCANO

You may have strong emotions that are about to surface. Can also represent fear that you will lose control in your waking life.

W

WALL

You may want to keep others away, or you may need to protect something.

WAR

Some inner conflict may be playing itself out in your dream. Do you feel torn about an issue or an emotion? You may have a desire to give up an attitude or defense mechanism.

WATER

A symbol for the self. Represents your unconscious mind. (See OCEAN.)

WEDDING

Suggests that opposite sides of one's self may be coming together, such as logic and intuition. Or you may simply want to get married.

WIND

A symbol of your spiritual, creative, or

life force. Can mean that you are on the brink of change.

WINDOW

Freud thought that a window was a female sexual symbol. Jung thought it represented a dreamer's attempt to understand the outside world.

WOMAN

For a man, an unknown woman in a dream can represent his psyche's attempt

to show the feminine qualities or
attitudes that may be helpful for him to
integrate into his personality. For a
woman, another woman may represent
herself. If the woman is unpleasant, the
dreamer may not like some aspects of
her personality. (See MOTHER.)

WOUND

You may feel hurt or betrayed by
another.

X

X-RAY

Suggests it's time to focus your energies on solving a problem. You're ready to look beneath the surface of a situation or problem.

XENOPHOBIA

A fear of strangers or foreigners can symbolize a fear of something in your own unconscious or personality.

Y

YACHT

May symbolize a desire for wealth, sea travel, or even a spiritual journey.

YARD

A backyard can suggest something hidden in your personality that you don't want to recognize. A front yard could represent the open side of your personality.

YACHT

Z

ZERO

A circle, this figure represents your whole, true self.

ZOO

May mean that you feel trapped or imprisoned, or that you have an instinct or trait that you want to free or keep locked away.